1998

For Lee White,
Because we
are all at risk,
We are able
to love.
Jim Bodeen
Sept 20, 1998

Impulse To Love

Impulse To Love

Jim Bodeen

Blue Begonia Press Yakima Washington

Acknowledgments—

In the Mari Sandoz Crazy Horse Camp *appeared as a broadside in* Wheel *from* Blue Begonia Press.
Ars Poetica *appeared in* Night Roses.
Letter to Rexroth from the Williams River, A Beginning in Silk, *and* Alone with the Trombones, *in* Footworks, The Paterson Literary Review, *where* Alone with the Trombones *received Honorable Mention in the Allen Ginsberg Poetry Contest.*
Thinking About Buckshot Kneaded in the Plastic C-4 of the Brain, World News, *and* At the Council of Churches Meeting on Just War My Townspeople Speak Up, *in* Crab Creek Review.
Literature in the World, *and* Hawks of the Midnight Sun, in Calapooya Collage, *by Tom Ferté.*
Sentries *was published as an original sHADOWmARK Broadside at* Blue Begonia Press.
A Bible Story *in* Washington English Journal.
Song of Juan Lagos *and* Reading Neruda's *Memoirs* Over Texas, *in* Borderlands 8 & 9.
Thinking Again of Mapuche Masks *in* Context South.
Reading Literary-Feminist Criticism *in* Gulf Coast.
The Birds *in* Seattle Review.
Letter to my Children: This is a War Story, *in* PoetsWest.
Ear Ache, Disappearing Into Blossoms, *and* In The Womb,
in the anthology , Bread For This Hunger, *where* Ear Ache *won First Prize in the poetry.*

Poems in Section II, The Price of Things,
were made possible by a Fulbright study exchange in Chile during the summer of 1991.
A sincere thanks to Ximena and David Hedrick; Kelly Ainsworth, International Programs at Central Washington University; Evergreen University; my colleagues who I traveled with, especially Sergio Bocas, my compadre, *whose knowledge of Chilean history and literature took me inside the history of words; Phil Garrison; Jim Rigney; Ricardo Chama; Marty Lovins who made possible the jewelry exchange; Barry Grimes, for the music before the journey; Bill O'Daly for his translations of Neruda's last works; Copper Canyon Press for making it possible to carry these translations to Chile; the people in these poems, especially Maria Catrileo, Juan Lagos, René San Martín, Mapuche* abrecaminos; *Don Eduardo, The* Machi; *the bookstores; the poets who must follow Neruda; and finally the Chilean people, poets all.*
Grateful acknowledgment is also made to the following places and individuals who assisted in making possible the completion of this manuscript:
Jane Schwab who handcarried the first poems; Linda Clifton who published them;
Wilderness Treatment Center; Abby of New Clairvaux; Pine Ridge Reservation; North Dakota Badlands; Center for Attitudinal Healing; A. J. Consultants;
National Endowment for the Humanities, Seminar on Biblical Narrative, Garrett Evangelical Seminary, 1995;
sHADOWmARKS;
Kevin Miller, for believing in the boy on the ice.
Avena Smith, Roland Dougherty, Wolfgang Roth,
Frank Malgesini, Karen Bodeen.

Cover Shield by Marty Lovins
Cover photograph of Shield, and photography on division pages by Rob Prout.
Book design and typography with assistance from Nancy Born
ISBN: 0-911287-27-2
Blue Begonia Press 225 So. 15th Ave. Yakima, WA 98902

For Karen,

&

For Tim, Krista & Leah

TABLE OF CONTENTS

I. Nothing Is Hid From The Heat

II. The Price of Things

III. Echoes

IV. Impulse To Love

IN THE MARI SANDOZ CRAZY HORSE CAMP
CEREMONY IS AS MATTER-OF-FACT AS FIRE
EVERYONE TRAVELS FROM A GREAT DISTANCE
THIS IS THE VISION FEATHER
MEN WITH THICK EARS CAN TELL WHAT HAS BEEN SAID
EARS FOR THE PEOPLE ARE A GREAT GIFT
EVERYTHING IS AN UNFINISHED STORY

We keep the strong Black Medicine, coffee.
We say no to whiskey.
We shed the fat of the soldier food.
We say no to things that divide us.
Someone will say something of the world behind this one.
This is why we have come.
We accept the fact that we are a broken people.
We have left people behind to come here.
Women go with the men they choose,
openly, untroubled, as is their right.
We do not turn our broken sides to each other.
The hearts of our women are not dust. We are not whipped.
We are shirt wearers. We are big-hearted.
The shirts show the solid world of our new life.
We will resist the reservation. We will not go in.
We are defenseless, but we are strategists.
We will use the earth for cover.
We are warriors. We have discipline.
Our enemies will not hurt us.
We are vigilant before our own people.
From defeat we have achieved a new fierceness,
a new kind of recklessness.
There can be no anger in the heart.
We will not stay here forever.
You learn how to go off by yourself.
You learn that you belong to others.

We have been shadow-marked.
Breathing together we cross through language.
Breathing together we cross through division.
No one can say what our work will be
when we belong to the people.
We will see like Crazy Horse.
And we will act like Crazy Horse.
Crazy Horse, remember, is a promise.
Crazy Horse is a very tough promise.
You want passion.
Beside passion everything is grass.

I. *Nothing Is Hid From The Heat*

Psalm 19

"THINKING ABOUT BUCKSHOT KNEADED IN THE PLASTIC C-4 OF THE BRAIN"—
—Yusef Komunyakaa

—January 14, 1991
for Roy Kokenge

Just suppose, Doc,
this seizure, this apoplexy,
is the claymore I carried home
from Nam. A woman
who works with my wife
thinks the Congressional vote
this week will set off
explosions with guys like me
all over the country.

And whatever my troubles,
let's not blame them on stress.
Republicans, maybe.
Anyone who talks in sound bites.
But not stress. And not cigars.
I'd consider bad religion.
Fifteen years ago
I had to study Lutheran theology
with Catholics because local clergy
didn't think the man in the pew
was ready for truth.
I bring this up because
the pastor's coming by later today.
And what about medicine?
It took four doctors to find out
I was blind in one eye. By the way:
thanks. That's why I'm writing.

I'm home today for the first time
in twenty years. Listening to music,
I've been thinking.
Where to lay the rap.
Listing my sins.
I don't think it matters.
If I'm hard on myself,
and it was me, I'd blame sins
I wanted to commit, but didn't.

Suppose it's these war poems
I've been reading.
Komunyakaa writes at the Wall:
Names shimmer on a woman's blouse
but when she walks away
the names stay on the wall.
We're all veterans of that one.
Wednesday you're going to ask me
about seizures. We'll talk
about the little explosions
going off all around us.

WORLD NEWS

—Then my soul froze.
Juan Rulfo

Everyone is dead.
All that is left are voices.
Voices everywhere
in Rulfo's spare prose.
Things have been bad for a long time.
And for a long time,
Rulfo, in Mexico,
has said nothing.

Now things are bad
in another part of the world.
There are voices
that won't go away.
They come into the living room,
through television,
bringing the past.

Echoes and voices.
A hospital ward full of NVA,
wrapped in bandages,
dripping blood. They have been
carpet bombed by B-52's.
I have never forgiven myself
for screaming.

Walter Cronkite tells
the reporter not to grandstand.
Things are bad. Worse
than Cronkite wants to hear.
Voices scare everybody.
Voices are the only hope we have.

AT THE COUNCIL OF CHURCHES MEETING ON JUST WAR MY TOWNSPEOPLE SPEAK UP

March 20, 1991
A small infant beginning to run.
—Muriel Ruckeyser

The Catholic Brother speaks first:
I think Augustine made a mistake.
I can't find Jesus' name anywhere
in the Just War Theory. Every time

the Church cuts a deal, Jesus gets
left out. Because he had walked around
the world thinking and thinking
of Augustine and Jesus, it rang true,

but it rang alone. Still, he knew
to be still. His voice had nudged us.
One woman said, My voice
was silenced by my neighbors cheering.

My voice was a small voice silenced,
another said. And another said,
This war has made war on my family.
This war isn't even over. It's a trick.

Don't feel bad because you believe in peace.
This is not the only war going on.
I'm not willing to join forces with Caesar.
I do not kill. I do not kill my neighbor.

And I do not kill my enemy.
But we sure do, we sure do.
What do we do in the face of such evil?
A woman who says nothing stands and bows.

A BIBLE STORY

I am six. Dressed in jeans
and a cowboy shirt. I am wearing
a gun on my left side, in a holster,
and hold my hat in my right hand.
I am fenced in. The fence
that surrounds me has seen years of weather.
It is a promise. Across the street,
Bethlehem Lutheran. A small town church
in a North Dakota town small enough
to match its isolation.
Armed only with story,
here I will be given David,
and David and Saul. I will hear
for the first time of Joseph
and how he is sold into slavery by his brothers.

Long after Bible translators have disposed
of the coat of many colors, I will hear
the Reverend Jesse Jackson call for a song,
Please now, the one who wears the coat,
call her up here, Sister Aretha,
a round of applause, for Aretha.
Even closer to where I live, a woman from Guatemala
will stay with us, in our home, and she will give me
her jacket, sewn by hand, in rainbow patches,
and I will wear it, marked, in my home town
among the stares of men, and the smiles of women,
and the women will say to me, entering the coffee shop,
Ah, the man who wears the coat.

Still, I will not know. The story will remain a story.
Marked, and blessed, I remain
on the outside of hope or knowing.
Egypt is what Anthony calls Cleopatra.

Egypt has been good to Joseph.
Yet his home is elsewhere. Wandering,
he becomes the Jew-to-be. Suffering
as his people suffer, he becomes
a swinging door to God. As his people
find a home, he will find a home with them. Still,

he will not be given any land. His bones
must be carried. Multicultural Joseph.
He must upstage his fellow actors,
and still expect his fellows to like it.
He wants to return to his father.
A monument in Egypt means little
compared to the monument in the hearts of people.
Joseph, Joseph, Joseph.
Masked man. Fenced out. Fenced in.
Dreamer turned bureaucrat.
Stocker of shelves for the famine in the human heart.

LEAVING THE MONASTERY WE WANT TO CROSS BACK SLOWLY, WE WANT TO CAMP, WE NEED A FEW THINGS, AND I NOTICE RIGHT AWAY, THE BABE, THE DUDE AND THE SPEEDBOAT

—for Janeen

I spot them right away. They're together.
The babe, the dude and the speedboat.
They're gorgeous.
Karen's driving and I have to say it.
I can't shut up.
Karen, look at the babe!
Karen, look at the dude!
Karen, look at the speedboat!
They're all so shiny!

I say to Karen,
If only I was a dude maybe
I wouldn't have to go through all this trouble.
Or, If only you were a babe and I was a dude.
It would be so easy. All I'd have to do
is get up and be a dude. And be shiny.
Gotta stay shiny. I know that.
If you're gonna be with the babe and the speedboat,
you gotta stay shiny.
If I was a dude I could keep myself shiny.
That goes with being a dude.

I look again at the babe. She is real shiny.
And the dude, too. Both of them shined
like that speedboat you can't hardly look at.

Now I start to get it. This isn't easy.
It's not easy being a babe. It's not easy being a dude.
If you're a babe you gotta be a babe.
You gotta be a babe all the time.
You got that dude because you're a babe.
He thinks you're a babe.
He believes you're a babe.
He believes it so much he got that speedboat.
He got that speedboat because he wanted to be a dude.
He maybe wasn't too sure what it was to be a dude.
Maybe he thought to be a dude with a babe
you had to have a speedboat.
Maybe he just wanted to be a dude, too.
I don't know. I didn't talk to him.
You don't just walk up and talk to a dude.
Dudes don't talk. Dudes aren't supposed to talk.
I know that from the get go.
He's got his hands full just being a dude.
I don't know how you get to be a dude.
I just know this guy, now, he's a dude.
And I can see it's hard work being a dude.
The world is a poor place to be so shiny.
And it's not easy being a babe and a dude.
It's not easy being a dude with a babe and a speedboat.
You just can't quit being a babe.
You just can't quit being a dude.
Even being a speedboat isn't easy.
When it shines, a speedboat
is something more that a speedboat.
How do you think a speedboat stays shiny?
You think a speedboat is God? Shines by itself?
Looking at the babe and the dude and the speedboat,
I know how hard it must be. People always looking at you.
You can never relax. You're a babe. You're a dude.
Maybe you're the speedboat. You gotta

keep on being what you are.
You can never quit shining.
Get up in the morning, look in the mirror,
you know what it is you gotta do, you gotta shine.
You gotta shine because you're a dude,
and you got a babe and a speedboat who shine,
and you will shine.

II. The Price of Things

In fact, the poem might be our only evidence that an event has occurred; it exists for us as the sole trace of an occurrence. As such, there will be nothing for us to base the poem on, no independent account that will tell us whether or not we can see a given text as being "objectively" true. Poem as trace, poem as evidence.

Carolyn Forché

Against Forgetting: Twentieth Century Poetry of Witness

READING NERUDA'S MEMOIRS OVER TEXAS

> *Comenzaré por decir, sobre los días y años de mi infancia,*
> *que mi único personaje inolvidable fue la lluvia. La gran*
> *lluvia austral que cae como una catarata del Polo, desde*
> *los cielos del Cabo de Hornos hasta la frontera, o* Far West
> *de mi patria, nací a la vida, a la tierra, a la poesía*
> *y a la lluvia. p.* 414
> —*Infancia y Poesia*

We're somewhere over Texas.
It's dry.
In Chile it's wet.
He recalls his first time
with a woman,
a man's wife,
anonymous, in braids,
she reaches out
for his young cock
as he lays sleeping
in the community hay
after a day's threshing.
She takes him there,
surrounded by harvesters
without a word,
without waking the men
tired from work.
The next day he looks
for her braids,
her covered breasts,
her anonymous lips.
He thinks he sees a smile.
Thirty thousand feet below me
it is all Texas,

dry, geometric.
I am flying to Chile
where it is winter, and rainy.
I am happy to be going now
to get a feel
for the rain in the poems,
to be rocked by events,
fire and water, wind and air,
surprising elements,
these things that will make
Neruda a poet
for those with no names.

FILLING UP AT THE MAPUCHE TABLE

Quise nadar en las más anchas vidas
—Pablo Neruda

—for Maria Catrileo

Already filled with crushed wheat
Mapuches call *catuto,* I know enough
to want to make this table mine. I step back
to fill up. While dancers snap handkerchiefs
to a Chilean *cueca,* a Mapuche cook fills my plate
with food passed hand to hand

for a thousand years. Stepping back,
I'm handed another *catuto,* this time
with chili and garlic. A child sings
songs of Violeta Parra and history is reborn.
The woman who crushed this wheat, rolling
it between two rocks, hands me a glass of *mudai,*

honey and wheat, fermented five days, not quite sour.
All is music and food. She fills our plates,
mine, and my friends who had never seen these stars
at night, and we peel *piñones* from an ancient
Aracanian bowl. Our plates refill
with *sopapilla,* Indian fry bread

back home; *kollof,* a seaweed boiled, then split,
with onions; *murkee,* toasted wheat that becomes
Ülpo when mixed with hot milk. Our host
has taught us the Mapuche word for poet,
Ülkantufe, noun of three languages,

charged to remember these names. No word

exists for cook, or teacher, actions too sacred
for even language. Food and song recall
the healer, *machi,* who enters the world of dis-ease
with his own map of many routes,
charting the dark course back to health,
table, back to this charged room

out of the pre-cordillera wind in Chile,
where our hands fill with story,
as well as wheat, where the other wine,
mixed with cinnamon and orange,
is called with wry Mapuche masks, *navigado,*
calling us home safe, but not quite straight.

AFTER 22 YEARS, TWO EMPENADAS FOR THE CHILEAN RETURNING HOME ON HIS BIRTHDAY

Ay, hijo que mal me pagas!
—Sign on the Cathedral

—for Sergio / 29 June 1991/ Santiago

So busy protecting two gringos
you don't think the gypsies
would get your last cigarettes.
This poem is a postcard for your wife:
Sra. Bocas, protecting us,
gypsies first took one,
and then the last pack
leaving your husband
desnudo of cigarettes,
and cursing in *La Plaza de Armas*
on his birthday, his second day home.

Sergio, the waiter doesn't care
any more for the empenadas
than he does for memory.
Today in *La Plaza* taking pictures
of the marble horse and rider,
kids playing beneath the legs
laughed us out of focus.
We take a taxi to *Calle Sin Salida,*
the dead end street where Neruda died
in the house he called *La Chascona,*
the messed-up hair, you recall for me,
remembering Don Pablo's love for metaphor,
chaos in all imagery. You try to bribe
the caretaker to get us in,

it doesn't work, we take pictures
of the graffiti, *Vive Neruda*, on the walk.
We ride to the top of *Cerro San Cristobal*,
and when singers come from mass
making traditional Chilean music,
spurs sparked like castanets,
and handkerchiefs snapping
in the quick fingers of women
excited the pigeons resting
in the Virgin's warm shade.

These things happen
before we run into gypsies.
You spot a stray dog,
teaching me another word,
Jim, *quiltro*, is a Chilean mutt.
Together we imagine empenadas,
the history of the last 22 years,
walking around Santiago,
waiting for a bus on your birthday.

HISTORY

Asi empezó la sangre,
la sangre de tres siglos, la sangre oceano,
la sangre atmosfera que cubrio mi tierra
y el tiempo inmenso, como ninguna guerra.
—Valdivia (1544)

In a river town it makes sense
to go back to the source.
And I only trust poets with facts
because they leave the rivers alone.
I cross the Valdivia on foot every day,
looking left at the country club
with its placid history of rowing,
and right at the fish market,
where fishermen concern themselves
with contaminated fish, the result
of decimated forests. When I arrive
at Andino's, the German-owned restaurant
off *la plaza de armas,* I take brewed coffee,
read *Canto General* and look out the window.
I read because nobody talks to me.
After three weeks the girl serving me only smiles.

On our last Sunday in Valdivia,
last night's wood smoke from the city
still lays on the river, curls
around the iron feet of park benches
in *la plaza;* a young woman comes up to me
and asks me if I will help her with her camera.

We are both so anxious to talk
that we begin taking pictures

and asking questions. She is a nurse.
She lives with her father.
She is waiting for her *novio,*
and his son. They are in love.
No, they will not be able to marry.
There are laws, bishops.
Yes, it is too bad.
But today the three of them will spend
the day together in Niebla
with his parents. It will be good.
When her *novio* comes we shake hands,
take pictures of each other.
Her question is to see what I'm like.
They leave before the weekly military parade.
I open up Neruda. I read again
about Valdivia riding into this place
and naming it, then dividing the land,
mi patria, among *ladrones,* thieves.
The long war with Mapuches begins with a single spade.

THE SONG OF JUAN LAGOS THE STREET SINGER

Así quiero que canten
mis poemas,
que lleven
tierra y agua,
fertilidad y canto,
a todo el mundo.
—Oda A Los Poetas Populares

Soy hombre del campo.
I come from the village.
I have nothing to teach. Nothing.
I defend the right to be born tomorrow.
I sing what I see.
Nothing more.
I don't invent.

Tengo gran amor para El Señor,
and my guitar, too.
I hope I don't offend the women.
No soy politico.
I have the land under my shoes, no more.

Soy hombre del campo.
Violeta Parra had to die
for us to know her.
I am not married,
but I have children.
Tengo todos los hijos
que no tienen padres.

All of the children
without fathers
are mine.

ONE ANSWER TO A QUESTION ABOUT MUSIC

Dónde está el centro del mar?
Por qué no van allí las olas?
—Libro de preguntas

The middle is also an extreme.
There is a loneliness
in the middle
drier than the Atacama.

I would have given my life
to kill Allende.
I would give my life now
to kill Pinochet.

We're tired of promises and lies.
We don't play that music anymore.
That music died with Víctor Jara
in the soccer stadium.

LITERATURE IN THE WORLD

Puse la frente entre las olas profundas...
—Las Alturas de Macchu Picchu

Down Chakabuko
away from the river

in the Chiloe bookstore,
Neruda's complete works

in two leather volumes,
a friend says. So we go.

They feel new. They are.
I hold this life's work,

all made 200 miles
from where I stand. After

being hidden 20 years.
A prison sentence, or

worse, for holding them
in your hand. Sergio

has his arms so full with
Quixote, he has to

sit down to open it.
The store, about the size

of this living room, holds
good books again. Sergio

wants this *Quixote.*
Then he goes quiet with

the clerk. "Jim," he says,
"turn around. Pinochet."

I turn, take one step,
put out my hand. Nothing

to say. Sergio does
the same. Shake hands, get out,

walk through his generals,
"Pure Aryan strain,"

Sergio whispers, into
stopped traffic and uzis

on *Chakabuko.* Neruda
took these guys on with words.

This man, Pinochet,
unleashed the forces

that shot up both
houses and poems

of a man who wrote twice
in "*Macchu Picchu,*"

"Sube a nacer
conmigo, hermano,"

who gave names,
Juan Cortapiedras,

Juan Comefrío,
Juan Piesdescalzos,

to the American
nameless, who first, more than

Whitman who he loved,
made us all Americans.

I question my handshake.
I hear this voice:

"There are people who we
must hate with our whole heart,

do good to them,
expecting nothing."

And I hear the American
Spanish of Neruda proclaim

a world *sin frontera,* that
Man is wider than the sea.

"Una vida de piedra
después de tantas vidas."

HAWKS OF THE MIDNIGHT SUN

—for René San Martin

I. Arriving

This medicine
of the *machi*

is not medicine
of today,

esta medicina
tiene mil años,

the young man says
holding up the urine

from his *suegro*
who has skin problems

German doctors
from Temuco can't heal.

The *Machi,* is man
and woman *al mismo*

tiempo, he says.
He is not *mágico,*

but he was born
knowing the culture.

He has been *Machi*

since 11 years old.

He is famous because
he knows who we are.

II. Learning

Blue makes us happy
because it is where

rain begins. But
there is too much rain.

Red is the flowering
of *el campo,* but

it is also aggressive.
Do you understand?

Bad spirits exist
with the good.

Machi protects
el pueblo.

Family is important.
Because we lived

only with family
we could fight

the Spaniards
for 300 years.

Your Hitler studied
Mapuche *guerreros.*

III. Beginning to Listen

It is not easy
to know the culture

so well that
one only fits

as *machi.*
The dream only says,

You're different.
Then you must be able

to say: I am.
I am *machi.*

Yo tengo
la capacidad

a ser curandero.
I value the pain.

Then I must act
to protect *el pueblo.*

IV. Going In

Going between
gods and *pueblo,*

la lucha con la fuerza mal,

bailen, cantan, tocan,

one must go with a map
and one makes the map

as he goes. All *machis*
know this. It is not

the map into dis-ease
that causes trouble

for *machi*. Anyone
can fall into

a sick mind. Trouble
comes with the *machi*

who doesn't have his map
back to *el pueblo*.

V. Machi Before the Fire

Reading the urine
of the sick, talking,

trying to find what
provoked the spirits,

this is from our fathers.
But as we sing

when we walk, we walk
on this road, under

these feet, we must

sing a new song.

Urine is part
of the ancient music

like this fire
in this *ruka,*

this thatched roof house,
with this ancient fire

on this dirt floor. We
are very far from

the banks and markets
of the cities

where we sit now,
surrounded by smoke

of this fire. I know this.
And like I know

our young people go
to the markets in Temuco

and Santiago, I know
what happens when

my people bring children
or fathers to the *ruka*

who are ill. We lay
them before the fire,

surround them with
this land you call Chile.

We have their families
and we have fire. The smoke

opens up time.
The family stands

and we beat the drum
and sing. When I go in

seeking the trouble,
Dungu Machife, beside me,

memorizes all
that I do. He knows

where I am. His map
will help me return.

I know something
of maps. I know

how far on the map
you have come to see

the *machi*. I know.
The maps are different.

It is all right.
I like your maps, too.

AFTER THE HEALING

René gives Don Eduardo *pan, vino.*
All the patients have gone home but us,
the gringos who arrive in two vans,
with umbrellas, notebooks, cameras,
to see the *machi*. René takes the stick
from Don Eduardo so he can eat.
He stokes the fire. We circle
the fire, around the *machi*.
This seeing goes both ways.
Machi wants the two *rubias,*
Karen and Jane, with their blond hair,
to sit next to him while we take pictures.
He asks if we'll send him copies.
Don Eduardo says he likes the fire.
He likes the attention too.
The shiny blue soccer jacket
he wears zipped to the neck
looks good connecting now and then,
with a white shirt collar pulled up around it.
His *pañuelo* ties his hair in a ponytail.
He tells David he's warming up.
He asks about weather in the U.S.
His assistant, a young teenager,
hands him *mate*. Jane gives him a chip.
David says camp is clean.
Don Eduardo says, Natural,
and points to the weave in the new roof.
Not knowing whether to turn into
eye or ear, I open myself to both
the smoke and the dark. I open
my notebook and whisper to my friends
to help catch scraps. René says,
It would be good to hear your song,

and Don Eduardo puts the *mate*
by the fire and laughs. He takes
down the drum from the wall, his hands
clean the leather drum painted with the four quadrants
of the world, warms the leather
before he plays, beginning with the stars painted
in the Southern Sky. He waits for René,
and then moves to the sun. Three times.
Four. Then he asks, in Spanish,
Cuando regresan a su país?
Then the stick, wrapped in colored yarn
takes over, and he responds by saying,
The climate will change when you leave.
He begins to sing the ancient iambic
rhythms of children. He plays on the stars
as he sings, his voice high-pitched,
a woman's voice, a long way off,
next to the proximity of the drumbeat.
Jenny, a young girl, maybe three,
walks up to him where he plays this song
handed on in dreams, and puts her head
on his lap by the drum, cutting her teeth
on the wooden edge of his chair.
Her ear, six inches from the drum,
makes me jealous. Then she smiles,
and I become a wave of sound.

Putting the drum down, René says
sometimes he sings for two hours.
Don Eduardo corrects him, saying,
Sometimes four. René agrees.
It depends on the ceremony.
Don Eduardo asks about his brothers
in our country. He wants to confirm
their red skin. *Piel rojo, distinto.*

And, *How are their lives?*
Nancy tells him about reservations,
and native history of *poco valor*
with our government. Don Eduardo
sits straight, skin tight over
an experienced jaw. At 46 years,
35 years of stories, 35 years of mapping pain.
Un piel, un sangre.
Somos mismos.
He says most *machis* are women,
and they marry, but it never works.
The husband is always jealous,
and he can never be as important as her work.
He talks about the power in the herbs,
and looks into the fire.
When he says, God knows
who is a *machi*, all of us circling this smoke
know we are all a long way from home.

July-August 1991
Temuco

BECOMING *"LECTOR CHILENO"*: READING "LAS ALTURAS DE MACCHU PICCHU" IN CHILE

Tus manos
fueron duras como piedras.
Tu corazón
fue un abundante
manantial de campanas.
—Oda A La Poesia

It doesn't happen until we leave
Santiago and go South,
where the rain
will open up the map
and every step and stone
will read like Chile.

New in Valdivia,
but outside Macchu Picchu,
I go into the poem
with two dictionaries,
a notebook, and the rain.
It's not an expected image
that emerges,
but a Chilean landscape:
air, rock, ocean.
Pueblo, root, rain.

The geography of loneliness
opens next, a fortress of rock.
A young man staring at the Southern Sky
tells me about his isolation,
an entire summer spent
walking ruins in Peru. And in spite

of *la aurora humana,* the roar
below from the *Wilkamayu,*
nothing changes.
He leaves as he came.

The sky's map throws us back
on the land. We marvel
at desert and wind,
we talk about *Macchu Picchu,*
and Neruda, Chile,
and the immense *cordillera*
of the human heart.

We drive through Puerto Montt.
I try to pick out the small hotel,
anonymous house, or face
that will hide Neruda
from his countrymen
while he searches
for a sheltered path through forests,
a forgotten Mapuche dream
over a carpet of *Copihue* blossoms
and exile in Argentina.

As our narrow boat ferries us
through canals on the way to Chiloe,
an *arco de iris,* doubled,
and complete on the water.

That afternoon, in a hotel in Ancud,
the poem opens up, I feel my face
facing the deep waves, going
down into the poem, a reader
approaching what the poet felt writing,
arriving like the brief crash of water

against rock, at myself.

Again and again I ask,
in this land where nature and man
deal headlines in horror,
going at it earthquake and machine gun:
How can it be that Neruda belongs to all?
How can it be, two generations of children raised
while poetry, music, burn as outlaws?

Fishermen and Communists nod,
quiet with me, becoming the poet:
Even the poet fails in his poem.
Fuiste también el pedacito roto.
This is an American song.

We know ourselves, momentarily, in the words.

Chile-Yakima
June-August 1991

THE PREACHER IN HIS LIVING ROOM

You have taken a bus to his house to listen.
You have been listening to him tell his story.
You have been listening like an athlete in top form.
You are, as they say, all ears.

The man is telling you about the knock on the door.
The *Campo de prisionero, Rondizzoni, Isla Quiriquna.*
You are receiving the story like a woman
receiving a man, and you want to hear this story.

The man is telling you about the *carcel* in Santiago.
His wife came here daily to ask about him.
She was told nothing. She was left each day to imagine.
And she couldn't talk. *No puede descutirlo.*

After 8 months the man is transferred to the island.
The man carves a camp from a board to prove he is here.
He has been called a *traidor de la patria.*
He will be here for two years. He will tell his story.

You will be in his living room to hear.
It will be many years later. You will sit and listen.
The man will call his wife and daughter into the room.
You will watch them as he tells his story.

You will wonder about them as they listen again.
You will look at them for signs. Maybe the story tires them.
Maybe the story changes. Maybe it is only a story.
The story has not yet made you afraid.

You will still be proud of yourself for being here.
For being such a good listener.
For opening your very body to the language.

You still believe the story will change the story.

You will be sitting on the couch all ears,
like the camera with the microphone held by your friend.
You will be like this when your friend asks,
in the kindest language you have ever heard,

about *la tortura,* the torture. Now you will be afraid.
You will hear the knock on the door now.
You will reach in your pocket for your passport.
It won't be there. You will remember sending out laundry.

You will think your passport has disappeared.
You will tell yourself how stupid you are.
You will cut deals to get out of this one.
You won't be listening so good now.

You will try to get out of this story.
You will pick up a book about reconciliation.
You will try to get out of this story
with a book. You learn fast now.

The book tells the same story.
It is the government's story of the government.
You will find the story of Victor Jara,
cantante popular. You will read the page

where the *Carabineros* meet him at the Theatre
and take him to the Stadium, where he will be shot
44 times, 32 bullets leaving his body.
Even as you read about the singer

you will not understand. You will not understand
because listening to the man in his living room
you were not able to hear the story.

You made yourself open and then you fell apart.

Later your friend will notice a photo of Neruda.
The man will say he came here often.
He will say he would eat olives and read.
He will say he wasn't very sociable.

Then you will remember the Neruda in your pocket.
You don't think it will help you.
You will think Neruda is just another poet.
You will be thinking about your passport.

But the man does not want you to go.
His family will bring out old pictures.
They will want you to stay longer.
Their story is a long story, a story

twenty years long, it will take a long time
to tell. Not many listen. Telling the story
makes him believe that all of this did happen.
All of this did happen.

You will be shown pictures of people
who have heard the story, of letters received.
If the man can make you believe his story
then it will have happened to you all.

for Pastor Jerry Carter
Calcohuirri, Chile

DRIVING TO ISLA NEGRA

Toda la noche he dormido contigo
junto al mar, en la isla.
—*La Noche en La Isla*

Out of Viña on a bus,
above the switchbacks
where new money
has put the new middle class,
I drive through cut forests
looking for you
in perforated Chilean sky.
I've crossed the page,
the voice I hear
dolorous, steady as the waves,
coming from my mouth is yours:
llegue a ser uno solo con mi tierra
conoci a cada uno de sus hijos.
Chilean rocks, cruza de piedras,
lapiz lazuli, backed with silver,
chained into bracelets
by artisans in Temuco
where you ran as a child
still free of poetry,
have been packed into my suitcase
for my wife and children.
I've been lugging this stuff
all over the South
carrying your poems,
all this landscape,
la persistente rosa
del litoral que vive con la espuma.
In a few minutes I'll face

your rocks at Isla Negra,
I try my voice again
to be certain what
I've just heard,
En medio de la noche me pregunto,
qué pasará con Chile?
Qué será de mi pobre patria oscura?

SENTRIES

...armados de una ardiente paciencia
—discurso del Premio Nobel

These poles surround the house of Neruda.
Tell the truth about these poles.
These poles are letters to the poet.
You will not be ready for these poles.

These poles take the wind's best shot.
These poles stand alone.
These poles are bound together.
These poles are ready for you.

These poles say things like,
Compañero, Pablo, el pueblo.
En noches como esta, te tuve
entre mis abrazos. These poles.

These poles have things to say.
These poles explain the economy.
These poles have taken bullets.
These poles did not go down.

These poles have long memories.
These poles do not belong to the university.
These poles are surrounded by rocks and waves.
These poles have friends.

These poles will ask for your help.
Dame un poco de tu espiritu.
These poles will cause you trouble.

These poles will make you want to speak.

These poles are a long way off.
These poles don't speak in riddles.
Cortaron las flores pero no
impidieran que llegue la primavera.

Don't be afraid of these poles.
Some of these poles are *desaparicidos.*
These poles will help you find yourself.
Do not be afraid of these poles.

for Ximena Spulveda & David Hedrick
Isla Negra, Chile/Yakima, Washington
July-August, 1991

A NEW DEAL FOR MASKS

Friends laughed when I told them
I was going to Chile to work on my mask.
Even in the first market
in Temuco, Mapuche masks
hacked out of tree trunks
with burned out eyes & nostrils,
mustaches of horse hair,
looked like political prisoners,
hung as they were
with the cheapest trinkets,
and I walked by
wearing my Fulbright necktie,
face cracking like cheap China
coming from an automatic dishwasher,
disgusted, pesos tight
in my money belt
around my waist under my shirt, smooth.

Every day I walked by those Mapuche masks.
Every time I saw the drill bit
making two more eyes, I straightened my tie.
Then on the last day, I bought.
Vance, Lovins and Grimes
are gonna get these Mapuche Masks
that don't show a thing
but contempt in the making.
The uglier the better for these guys, I thought,
these guys, these handsome friends,
these men who work the interior world,
building the inner face, everyday.
"Give me three of those Mapuche masks," I said.
"Yes, those, the ones by the whistles."

SIXTEEN FULBRIGHT FELLOWS HELPING OUT IN CHILE

It is winter, and wet,
in Chile, real wet,
but the sixteen
Fulbright Fellows
from Washington State
have our umbrellas.
We know about rain.
We're ready to help.

We're pulling up now
in four taxis, sixteen of us.
Yes, here we are.
Now we're getting out of the cabs.
We're unfurling our umbrellas.
We know how to stay dry.
We know how to go native.
And we're here to help.

Let's get these umbrellas up.
Now let's go look at these schools.
It must be hard to teach without any books.
Can you tell us about it?
We're here to listen.
Let us put these umbrellas down.
Let's talk frankly.
You can tell us.
We know how tough it must be,
but tell us.
We can be trusted.
We're here to help.
That's great.
Tell us more.
But hurry.

We have appointments.
In 30 minutes we have an appointment
for lunch with the mayor.
He's going to tell us how we can help.
He's going to tell us how we've helped so far.
He's going to tell us how tough it is.
And we know it's tough.
Yesterday we rode the bus
through Santiago. We saw.

Not everyone has an umbrella.
Some people are out in the rain.

And 17 years of government repression.
17 years of General Pinochet.
17 years of teachers not being able to teach.
17 years of censorship.

Tell us what it was like.
Tell us how tough it must have been.
Were any of your family imprisoned?
Tortured? Disappeared?
Tell us please. Please tell us.
We're here to help.
We're American.
We're Christian.
We're Fulbright Fellows.
We're here with our umbrellas.
And we're here to help.

AMONG THE POLITICOS IN VALPARAISO

no acabas
de peinarte,
nunca
tuviste
tiempo de vesterte...
—Oda A Valparaiso

A man can't quit being a *payaso,* a clown,
but he can change his necktie. Thirty
minutes ago, walking with penguins
over rocks in a downpour, looking
for plankton that didn't get out with the tide,
my umbrella up, but not keeping out water.
Valparaiso, my one necktie is in rags,
electric neon corn husks poorly wired,
but blinking, FRAUD, FRAUD, over my chest.
I take my official portrait among these rocks.

Diplomacy is for others. I came to Chile
looking for Neruda. Yesterday, letters
and poems written by the pilgrims
on the fence posts at Isla Negra,
shattered what was left of my mask.
It's a democratic world and the general's
in charge. I'm finished, no use trying
to hide. Governments have grown honest,
there's nothing more straight clothes can do for me.
Yo soy huaso, a cowboy in cowboy clothes.

Bussed to a law school,
or maybe it's not a law school,

maybe it's city hall, I fold up my umbrella,
give up all pretense of *Castellano,*
start talking in broken Mexican.
Taking coffee with two lawyers from the New Right,
I ask them if they know Neruda's Ode to Valparaiso.
Valparaiso, my half-dressed friend. They don't,
and I say, "Why don't we read it together."
And standing there before the political forum
on the new democracy, that's what we do.

Valparaiso, half-dressed, when tremors hit.
A disheveled city naked in colored shorts
and tattooed belly, surprised with death,
hanging on with your fingers, rocked
by waves and rocks. Lawyers laugh.
delighted with their city on the page,
delighted with repetition, hard c sounds:
camisa...calzoncillos...con flecos de colores,
and the vowels Neruda called colored stones,
glittering, that "leaped like silver fish,"
lawyers love that, seeing their city
through Neruda's eyes for the first time,
maybe asking themselves later,
"We shot up his house for this?"

You, their city. Like getting photos
back from Kodak, passing them around. And just
that fast, bankers' houses tremble
like beached whales wounded, trembling.
The house of the poor jumps a ditch
like a caged bird freed, tipping its hat.
Pronto, Valparaiso, putting tears behind you,
you rebuild, repaint, a transformed ship
indestructible, a far star in the night,

hope, struggle, solidarity, and happiness
tattooed to your southern chest. "*Como*
anclas que resisten las olas de la tierra."
A tough and stubborn anchor, Valparaiso,
hanging on. Houses built piggyback,
my stomach and chest collapse while reading,
poverty spills from hills like water.
Lawyers in love, Neruda walking them
through Valparaiso. We finish the poem,
politicians talk and get sober again.
We are in the serious room, talking serious.
But it is already too late for me. My umbrella
is down, the knot in my tie a failure.
The language will take you to lawyers or Neruda.
You can only choose one.
You must stand in the rain
and choose for yourself.

THE SONG IS A TWENTY YEAR CHAIN

—Would we have stayed to an end or would we have folded our faces?
Awful and awful. Good friend. You have embarrassed our hearts.

from Miller Williams' "For Víctor Jara: Mutilated and Murdered,
the Soccer Stadium, Santiago, Chile"

September 15, 1974

In this anniversary year of the murder of Víctor Jara,
Chilean poet and popular singer,
the U. S. Postal Service plans to issue
the Richard M. Nixon postage stamp.
I believe in horror. Perhaps you've noticed,
American citizen, how the powerfully benevolent
deny connections made by our own minds,
returning us numb to doubt and denial.
In January you will be licking Richard Nixon's face.
Try acting outraged about this stamp in public.
Recall one of Nixon's lies you have not yet
forgiven and check the local response.

Several years ago I discovered myself in Chile,
waking from a deep sleep. Months earlier
I woke up paralyzed on one side of my body
and blind in my right eye. Recovering my sight
I discovered myself to be uncovering things
my family had told me could not be dignified by speech.
My family loves me. I carried Neruda with me
wherever I went, I listened to the Mapuches
in Spanish and let the gaps in understanding

fill up with the missing holes in my own story.
I bought music that had disappeared.
I heard stories so frightening
that I didn't recognize them as my own.

The World Cup comes to the United States.
Pasadena is the home field of the Americans.
That's what we call ourselves before the world,
the Americans. In the first exhibition game
against Mexico, 90,000 Mexicans
living North of the border
show up to cheer the old country.
The American team is shocked.
In their own stadium they have no fans.
Two months later Californians
pass a law cutting out medical aid
and education to any without papers.
Teachers and nurses promise
to break the law. I drop a cassette
into a music machine that produces sound
as clean as wind in the Andes.
In their loneliness, mountain and wind
call across time for flutes, until finally,
imitating wind and mountain, men learn
to blow into hollowed reeds and make music.
Víctor Jara sings.
Isabel Allende lives with us now.
She's writing about us, too. She's got us down.
In Chile I kept asking about her stories, critically,
continually, discounted by universities.
I couldn't see I had no right to her truths,
the family story. All countries are small.

Now poets talk about writing the perfect poem.
That's what they do, write perfect poems.

(Now we listen to altaplano music to relax.)
Now Víctor Jara's songs, innocent of our horrors,
call us back to an innocence we still must call denial,
still able to say, No, no, never,
not for songs such as these. Not possible.
He sings, he still sings, *Abre la ventana.*
One doesn't have to know the language
to get the message. This is music.
The price of things, the cost of song.
We'd rather talk about someone else's country.
We'd rather talk about the country than ourselves.
Quiet songs explode with everything we've feared:
The last 25 years of the 20th Century.
Love, literature, music, painting, photography.
The human body itself, each, all, politicized.
Genocide begins as a family secret.

Chile finally publishes the Retig Report.
Informe de la Comisión Nacional de Verdad y Reconciliatión
So family members will know what happened.
To their children.
I take photos of the two volumes on the wall in my room.
I set a coffee mug at their side on the chair
so that my memory will not mistake their size.
Two volumes thick as city phone directories
listing, in alphabetical order, the disappeared in Chile.
For the American memory, citizen, read with me:

Víctor Lidio Jara Martinez, 40 años. Cantante popular y director teatral, miembro del Comité Central de las Juventudes Comunistas. Víctor Jara fue detenido el día 12 de septiembre en el recinto de la Universidad Técnica del Estado, lugar en el que prestaba sus servicios como director teatral, siendo conducido al Estadio Chile, donde tras ser separado de los demás arrestados junto a él, fue mantenido en los altos de una galería, junto a otras personas consideradas como peligrosas. Entre el 12 y el 15 de ese mes, fue interrogado por personal del Ejército. El 15 de septiembre es el último día en que se le vio con vida, cuando en horas de la tarde Víctor Jara fue sacado de una fila de prisioneros que serían traslados al Estadio Nacional. Al día siguiente, el 16 de septiembre, en la madrugada, su cuerpo fue encontrado en las inmediacones del Cementerio Metropolitano por unos pobladores, junto a otros cinco cadáveres, entre los que se hallaba el de Littré Quiroga Carvajal. Conforme expresa el informe de autopsia, Víctor Jara murió a consecuencia de heridas multiples de bala, las que suman 44 orificios de entrada de proyectil con 32 de salida. La Comisión se formó la convicción de que el afectado fue ejecutado al margen de todo proceso, constituyendo ello una violación a sus derechos fundamentales de responsabilidad de agentes del Estado. Funda esa convicción en que se encuentra acreditado el arresto así como su presencia en el Estadio Chile; que se halla acreditada su muerte por una gran candidad de heridas de bala, lo que demuestra que fue ejecutado junto a los demás detenidos cuyos cuerpos aparecieron junto al de él. Las torturas a que fue sometido Víctor Jara durante su detención se relatan en la Parte General de este periodo.

44 bullets enter the body and 32 bullets exit.
This is the story of the singer and the soccer stadium.
This is the story of the Richard M. Nixon postage stamp.
This is my story of how I began waking up in Chile.
It's a story about music. A love story. About our family.
It is not a perfect story. You have a story.
Maybe one time someone told you not to tell it.
Maybe you did what you were told. That time.
It's one more song. It's still there. It's your bullet.
You don't have to be a citizen to tell a story.

III. Echoes

O, what is it in me that makes me tremble so at voices.
Walt Whitman

Yes, the village is full of echoes. They don't scare me anymore.

Este pueblo está lleno de ecos. Yo ya no me espanto.
Juan Rulfo

BOWBELLS, NORTH DAKOTA: GETTING THERE

Tucked up in the NW corner.
Don't take the Interstate.
Easier to come through Montana
or down from Canada.

People driving to Bowbells
are coming from a far place,
birth place,
or returning from some place,
with provisions,
Minot or Williston,
if they're still in Bowbells.
Seattle and the West Coast
for those who left for good,
who could get out,
but couldn't stay.

When you're there
you can't see it.

When you leave
you can't let go.

When you come back
you can't find it.

My mother told me
to take Highway 85 out of Williston.
Go 14 miles and turn East on 2,
go 32 miles through Ray to Stanley.
The Tioga oil fields
will be on your right, to the North.

At Stanley go North on 8
through Lostwood and Coteau.

You will know you're close
when you see signs: Lignite,
Portal, Northgate, Fortuna, Flaxton,
Hamlet and Wild Rose.

THE MAN AND THE BOY ON THE LAST DAY OF THE YEAR

The Man Returns And Finds The Boy

Just give me a hug
North Dakota boy.
Just give me a hug.
After all this time.

Full of all the loneliness in North Dakota.

From now on time won't matter.

We can get angry later.
We can get mad now.
Whatever you need.
Whatever you want.

Can you believe in now?
For now.
It doesn't matter who left you.
What matters is who
came back to get you.

40 years is a long time
for a little guy to have to wait.

The Man Asks 3 Questions

Sitting here with you
I don't know who I am.

You tell me.

Am I your father
or your big brother?

Or,
this sounds crazy,
am I you?

Together In One Body

No love? None?
For all these years.

No wonder you turned tough.

You turned tough quick.
The tough guy made it possible
for you to wait.

I'm here.
I'm only here for you.
I don't know
if there are limits
for us.

Who's to say what's right
for two guys in love,
who live in the same body,
who've been separated
for as long as you and me?

Being here for you

is the same thing
as being here for me.

Some Of The Things

All the trips back.
More trips than a trucker makes.
Count them.

Sometimes I wouldn't even see people.
Sometimes I wouldn't spend the night.
Just look around.

Go to the cemetery.
Ask a stranger a question.
Try and hear something in his voice
and drive back to the coast.

Lost in the world where I'm known,
where I'm husband and father,
where I plant flowers,
suddenly all these trips make sense.

I'm looking for you.
The little boy left behind.
The left child.
The one that didn't get out.

Jimmy Bodeen. North Dakota boy.

Fragments scattered in grass,
wheat never harvested,
spilled grain
never chewed into flour,
made into bread.

Shouldered with a man's story
before you had a man's heart.
A woman's story.
You took your mother's voice
years before the family left.
It was already yours.
Given to you before you had a choice.

What The Man Told The Boy

Oh, you took it.
You took it good.
You never knew
what it was until now.

Your mother's story.
Your mother's pain.
Not just your mother's.
Any woman's.
Any beaten person.

That's what you didn't know.

What The Man Did Next

There's plenty of time
for that stuff later.
Let's just hold on now.
Let's just hold each other.

The man holding the boy.
The boy holding the man.

The two of us
in the same body.

Give me the woman's story.
Go play. Be a boy.
It's easier knowing you're alive.
I thought you were gone.
This is no story for a boy to carry.

December 31, 1993—January 6, 1994

THE MAN AND THE BOY

I searched everyone.

I've been looking in everyone for you.

I never existed.

What looked like me disappeared.

I didn't disappear to survive.
I was gone.
What was left could be cute.
What was left could get attention,
but I was already gone.
My first memory is my grandma's
telephone number, 29.
Even this call for help was long distance.

I remember that, too.

I remember Grandma talking about you.
She said, You can always come here.
You can always come to Grandma's.
She said she'd watch you
from the kitchen window,
"come trudging up the driveway
no bigger than a minute."

Yes. I could always go there.
I belonged at Grandma's.
And I belonged in Grandpa's truck.
And the railroad tracks
on both ends of town.

Both sets of tracks were mine.
I was a boy in a mask.
I was the town boy
in a farmer's town.
I was a whip,
and I covered the town
in fast smiles.

You had a camp in a grove of willows
out past Shit Creek on the Great Northern Tracks.

I believed it was a Sioux burial site.
The rocks were too beautiful.
Only God could have placed them.
Or grandchildren. Grandchildren
would have taken the time
to place them like that in those trees.
They would do that for a grandfather.
I smoked Indian tobacco here.

I smoked a peace pipe from a souvenir store.

I still can't believe you.
How can you tell me this
and then say you never existed?

I never came into being as me.

I had hockey skates.
I skated on the ice at Shit Creek.
I wrapped my ankles in the rich
brown and black leather.
I was never a figure skater.
I carved my balance

on the ice, alone,
under the tracks
carving ribbons of ice.
My breath mirrored
the tracks in the ice,
escaping into the ice blue
January sky over North Dakota.

I turned into a blue ribbon
in school by reading Dr. Seuss
and I was gone, disappeared.

You became a clown?

I only lived on the skin.
The surface of the world
became the field where I could feel.

A child's body can't protect its spirit.

You're still talking about yourself.
You don't get it, do you?

I was harder on myself than anyone.
Aren't you happy I'm here?

You sound like our mother.

You don't get me because even then I was gone.
I was a six-year-old Sioux Indian
smoking a peace pipe by the railroad tracks.
I became the disappearing echo of drums.

I can't get behind the drums.

When the child died, the baby,
my spirit was born in this boy.
I was an Indian on a bicycle.
The railroad tracks were promises.
Even the town.

I had grandparents.
But even in this story
I had been left behind
by my own people.
Even my only story of home
wouldn't last. I would lose this, too.
The boy would be thrown out
with his parents. Now
you've found me in this North Dakota wind.

We do belong to each other.
We are each other.
I am you. You are me.

Maybe so. But I am nothing.
I have nothing to say.
It's not that I'm bitter. I'm empty.
You have the heroics of all you've done.
I am not even the sound in the wind.
You can try to love me.
You can't wrap your arms around me.
I am not something you can hold.
You can have no expectations.
I am this emptiness.
It is all that I am.

EAR ACHE

Covering my ears,
I am on the blue couch,
a boy,
hoping the pillow will take the pain,
calling for the next level of intensity
that will bring the drill of relief.
I believe in the warm oil
dropped into my ears.
I believe in the darkness
of the moment of sleep.
I believe in the pain.

I am wrong about my memory.
Mom tells me I had ear aches
before I had language.
Mom tells me I heard things
I shouldn't have heard.
She remembers coming home from work
too tired to listen herself.
I used to give you kids
a quarter each day for not telling me
what went wrong. I told you too much.
You heard things.
You heard things before you were born.

I walk in the garden.
The flowers are all ears.
I am struck by the nurturing blossoms,
by the voice in each petal,
by all this listening,
by so many syllables forming flowers.
I am surrounded

by so many words and stories.
How one can be alone
and hear so much!
From simple listening.
Exhausted, music comes again.
To be a mouthpiece for Orpheus.
Flowers of a deeper soil.

This is the ear's report.
Sometimes music arrives this way,
in a North Dakota winter wind
whistling through a child's ear.
A child still too young to speak.
This is the miracle of music and flowers.
It is grass. It gives up undetected blossoms.
This is a mother's prayer,
whispered into her child's ear,
that she be heard.
This is all that she has said.
She has given her son a story.
The aching is only love.

DISAPPEARING INTO BLOSSOMS

I looked into everything
that had disappeared.
I had to disappear myself.
My search for you, North Dakota boy,
took me outside and far away.
I rested in poems.
I moved into the negative space of others.
This was not a home but a way.
I didn't know that.
I'd place myself within earshot
of any voice promising a story.
I'd wait for a voice to move into.
I did this until it knocked me out.
Locked me right out of myself.
I couldn't get back into my own skin.

Now I've found you.
But where are we?
Even with the map
of these poems
and the directions
in all the voices.
It's not that we're lost,
the two of us,
it's that this search,
this traveling into ourselves,
makes us lonelier in returning.
Even in coming back
we're going on.
Our treasure is not
the music of Orpheus,
it is in the flowers.

IN THE WOMB

Already I'm listening,
carrying her story.
I have it all. I take it all inside
when I am still connected.
I am given everything
before I have a chance
to choose. All of it.
Given then. Then spend
my life looking for it.
In front of me all the time.

I need the story
that must be told
in its own pure voice.
I listen. I take it all.

I go looking
because that's what
makes me real.
I see my mother's handwriting
in my baby book.
Jesus didn't cry when they put
the nails in his hands.
I have been given all this.
An inheritance.

This is a children's story.
I tell, too.
What the child hears.
What children hear.
There are many of us.
We're not alone.

Each time,
each time a story is heard,
the world comes clean.
I go looking for stories,
stories to listen to.
I still need them.
I still hear the story given to me.

My telling is this—
a way to tell my mother
she has been heard.
Listening and telling
are the same thing.
I can't tell what I haven't heard.
Everything was told to me
in the beginning.

AND VOICES
ALWAYS COME INTO THE WORLD
IN TIME TO SING,

Each stone I overturn
in every North Dakota field
is an abandoned child
recovered and given to the world.
Faith doesn't depend on me,
but on God. Give it up.
Now I know. I hear you.
You're nurturing a voice.

IV. Impulse to Love

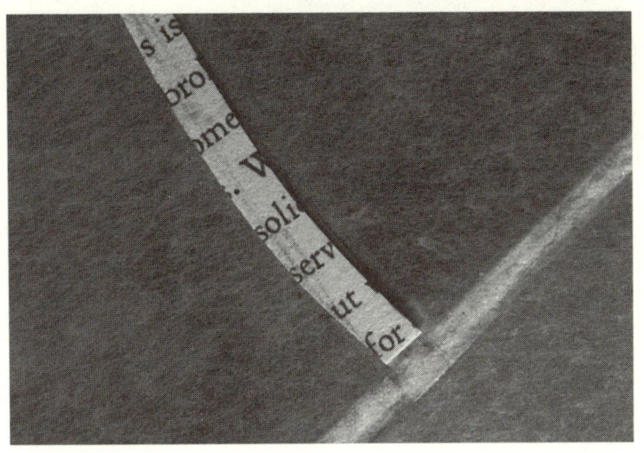

...sweeter also than honey
and drippings of the honeycomb.

Psalm 19

Ars Poetica

My brother asks on my birthday
if the lawn job I had in junior high
had anything to do with this garden.
Harry Reinarder gardened blind
the last ten years of his life,
and walked me through the rhodies
and azaleas before he paid me.
Thanking my brother for his praise,
I recall almost giving in to darkness.
Harry made sure I knew
the importance of the cool shade,
the acid in the soil. *Here*
is the secret of azaleas, he'd say,
blossoms lighting up our way
on paths of lifted beds.
Here, solace is here.

ALONE WITH THE TROMBONES

—for Walter Brueggemann, Phyllis Trible & Jonathon Kozol

Arguing with the newspaper
over one minute of light on solstice,
using the paper's own facts,
I know the short ride is always the long one.
I hear trombones and voices.
A rich man names his daughter Tiffany.
A girl in the Bronx is called Eternity.
I carried a trombone a mile to school
during five years of my life
when I could hardly go out in public.
It's funny. Eternity is not a laughing matter.
I was never a wizard with the slide.
Don't slur. Play the positions.
Roll along, prairie moon.
The trombone knows how life treats those
who wear their hearts on their sleeves.
Look up and there's Jeremiah.
I was so far from jazz I fell in with outlaws.
They gave me the trombone after third grade
because they needed marchers in the high school band.
This was North Dakota. They gave my cousin Sharon
the french horn. We left for Seattle looking for work.
My dad sank rivets in airplanes.
I carried the trombone through the suburbs.
Boys quit talking to me. I never knew what it was.
But I was carrying that trombone.
Walking down the same street. The other side.
Music. So this is God,
lost embouchure, old recordings. Look up.

Phyllis Trible and Walter Brueggemann tap their feet.
Life's little ironies. Jonathon Kozol gets on a subway.
Cadences fall with the natural ease of speech.
I don't know a single woman who plays trombone.
The burry smear, the growl. Bass cleft.
I never said one kind word about the trombone.
Miff Mole, Tommy Dorsey, Jack Teagarden.
I played gospel in the living room.
I could make my mother cry.
The trombone is smooth, like whiskey.
It would calm my father's rage.
What I never loved in public, myself,
all went into hatred of that trombone.
J. J. Johnson, Jimmy Cleveland, Walter Lewis.
Awkward, clumsy, virtuosity, all crammed inside.
The saxophone could squeal.
The mouthpiece. Metallic kisses.
White shirt and tie. The living room concerts.
The man who prays for Eternity is a Jew.
In heaven you pay for things in smiles.
Someday there will be a meadow for children.
This is the rebirth of light.
Not a minute. Not an exile.
A life in a song. A home in a note that holds.

WATER, PAINT, LEAVES

With pitfalls to shun, guides to follow, provisions to use.

—Phyllis Trible

One day the gardeners walk away, quit.
The great painter's vision isn't worth the effort.

A woman with another vision of beauty
hands out an invitation to terror.

A man raking leaves listens to a football game
on the radio. Monet has a road paved

to reduce dust on the lily pond
to bring the landscape closer to his eye.

This is terror, not reflection. The man
raking leaves remembers the woman

who brought him the last zucchini
from her garden. The suffering

at my side is not subordinate
to the suffering of the cross.

A splotch of color. An impression
made on the retina. Evil is the organism's

capacity to resist its own growth.
The marine says keep your Silver Star.

Yet we hold on, seeking a blessing.
The invitation is to assume all risk.

OCTOBER PRAISE FOR MY FRIEND WHO WRITES

—for Tim Carpenter

All travel is good, especially the traveling
one does staying home. Take Montana, take Greece.
If I could build a home in my heart
I wouldn't need to build a cabin in another state.
Another state. I'm in another state.
It's early, Sunday morning, October 1.
I read a book that tells me,
Death is a reminder that this life is limited, precious.
Life reminds us this about death.
No one idea gets it all.

When I think about recovery,
I think the practice of life is Buddhist.
Yet the language is street Christian.
Clichés of Christ may one day turn up
in a sand cave near Qumran.

Remember the temples in Vietnam?
I wondered at all the color.
I wondered how to worship.
I marveled at these buildings without walls.

I always made the driver stop.
Have him pull the jeep
alongside this sky temple
and ask questions. I liked

being in fatigues, getting away
from the hospital, surrounded by
the fact of rice paddies. The beauty

of an underwater crop for a boy from

North Dakota who knew wheat
and the miracle of dryland farming.
Vietnam shapes us today.
Four Vietnamese women will walk by

my garden this morning on their way to Mass.
A grandmother, the mother, two daughters.
I will cut flowers. We won't talk.
We won't count the loss.

I'm a master at counting what's been lost.
Grieve everything. And praise.
What I do to keep from praising
keeps me sick. This morning's paper
attacks those who work the Psalms
with new contexts for our times.
The Lord is my shepherd.
Stephen Mitchell translates,
I have everything I need.
And David Rosenberg's Blues of the Sky reads,
and keeps me from wanting what I can't have.

I have everything but can't see it in my grief.
I have so many flowers I can't see my own.
Enough. Abundance in enough.
Longer silence between words.
And your letters traveling in the mail.

CLEANING UP THE YARD

...the grand god revealed himself, sounded, and went out of sight.
—Moby Dick

All night long the cat cried
missing my daughter.
Finally my wife lets her out.
I refused to respond to her cries
even though I was awake
unable to sleep.
And I woke up carrying this phrase
about cleaning up the yard.
Death is an ally.
All spiritual people are hyphenated.
When I came downstairs
the cat had made a mess
all over the rug. I cleaned that up.
How odd, I thought, at any moment.
The yard is clean.

It's still dark.
Waiting for the coffee
I cut up my sheet of school pictures
into individual plates.
A 50-year-old man.
I am wearing a t-shirt
designed by a friend,
a left-handed calligrapher,
for his wife, a potter.
Rimless bifocals,
and for the first time in my life,
long hair.

I ran Med Evac in Vietnam.
85th Evac Hospital
in Qui Nhon. On the South China Sea,
South of Danang. Took guys off choppers
and 123's. Got them out.
Far away and fast. Sometimes
before they woke up.
I was incountry
when Lieutenant Calley
shot up the ville. We took in
those casualties. On both sides.

My friend in the 4th Division
came in with his First Sergeant
and we were drinking beer
in the club when Top pulled out
his knife and went over the table
after a guy who said something
about me I didn't catch.
Top was screaming,
Nobody fucks with the Bo.
It was like this for six or seven months.
Around the clock.
Chopper blades for second hands.
My friend went home before
it was over. His little brother
killed himself in Seattle.

These things come to me
in the flowers. These beds now.
They're my life. Make good beds
is what I do. After I dig out
river rock, I sift dirt for stones,
leave nothing more than pebbles.

I've been wondering
what happened to those college kids.
I came home in August of '68.
I was married and on a college campus
in January. Those kids asked me
two questions. How many babies
did I kill and did I have any dope.
And you know I saw those babies.
And their mothers too.
Ones that were under those B-52's.
We wrapped them in gauze
until they disappeared.

After the bombing stopped
we had a ward for everybody but us.
They sent us back to the United States.

FOR THE WOMAN WHO WANTED MORE BUT WOULD NOT LOVE US

You've been to Vietnam and there's no horror in your voice.
—The woman

Where were you in 1968?

The music is Mahler. The 3d Symphony.
Those are children singing.
They will die later in the song.

The soldier moved by love
does not deny his impulse to kill.

LITERARY-FEMINIST READINGS OF BIBLICAL NARRATIVES

—for Nancy Haught

Your voice takes me effortlessly into texts of terror.
I carry Phyllis Trible from August through October.
Sad stories are taking on new beginnings.
I end up again in Vietnam.
I see a story denied since 1968. A love story.
An unbroken line goes under the language.
Sympathetic readings of abused women
don't turn us into victims—
they redeem the time. Casting off
the need for a compassionate God liberates us.
I don't need the patron in my head.
I get the message: With the sweat of your forehead
you shall produce fruits. Share the fruit, not the sweat.

Clean scholarship of Trible lays out before me
the form of rhetorical criticism until the story breaks open.
Repetition, verb choice, ring narratives,
serve to slow us down until our seeing
becomes political action. This is poetry when poetry matters.
The story teller puts herself at risk telling the story.
I hear myself talking, *I don't know if I can do this.*
I don't have any choice.
What makes this truth happen when the feminine leads?
Danger knocks at the door of merriment.
I take Trible's lines at random, drop them into poems.
She is property, object, tool, and literary device.
I haul scrapbooks up from the cellar.
The slave Hagar moves toward being.
The grieving Tamar claims her voice.
Women who recover their stories

redeem the time voice by voice.
Terror turns into music. This is Nam.
One tries again to uncover the love
in each impulse. Here is a beating heart.
Blood pumping from each severed limb
gives itself up in hope.

TO MY CHILDREN: A WAR STORY

I never got over the college kids.
A month after I came home
I was on a college campus,
surrounded by kids who said how bad we were.

Because I knew how bad it was
I forgot how much love we gave, how we worked
to heal anyone hurt. And we were good.
No casualty would be denied our love.

We were ready for each chopper.
Each plane loaded with casualties
confirmed our ability to love.
We never shut down, ever.

This is a war story. We were good.
I denied it all the first day back in school.
The cost of not believing in my mission?
This is a war story:

The day I quit believing in me,
I could never be good enough again.
Someone always cared more, thought more,
believed more. I believed like this.

I went to war for peace, even as I quit
believing in the peace I worked for.
College kids believed we were wrong,
and they had my attention. I knew more,

and didn't. I couldn't forgive them

because I couldn't forgive myself.
I got as much from the war I brought home
as the war I embraced. Tough enough

for love. It's a good song.
The bishop tells me every breath
comes from God. I couldn't see it,
until I broke the back

of my own betrayal of me. Evil
is an impulse of love breathed wrong.
The flip side of all we are is good.
Every act is an act of love.

Love, Dad

THE BIRDS

...fluttering over the water there, wheeling round and round, with joyous expectant cries. Their vision was keener than man's.
—Moby Dick

Praise their song. And praise their nervous flight.
Praise them for they see danger.

My friends are hard stars in the dark night.

When the big fish begins to surface
the birds swirl and swirl.

Today is the Day of the Dead.
A cross-quarter day, halfway between
autumnal equinox and winter solstice.
A woman has sent me two bouquets of flowers.
One vase contains two artichoke buds
that will never open, mixed with fall grasses
whose beauty will remain until spring blossoms.

A man gives me two poems.
The man himself is one of them—a captain of light.
Rested, not resting, winnowed from the past,
whirling in a disinterested orbit of hard energy.
There are birds everywhere,
on the move, scuffling, some just moving—
but moving! Birds and saints
complete their purposes.

I have paid great tribute to the big fish,
fearful of the birds, and contemptuous.
What neglect of their royal watch.

Praise the birds.

CANYONLANDS AND ALL SOULS' DAY

—for Vance

What Mexicans give to Halloween confuses
many of the citizens in Yakima. Celebrated right,
one spends more for food & drink
on the Day of the Dead than for gifts at Christmas.

And the dead eat first, after fireworks
clear the debris in the cosmos. The living
eat the extravagant leftovers while learning
to say thanks, and mean it. Vance,

300 Mexican kids knocked on our door
wearing masks, beginning this 3-day binge,
and Yakima thinks they're beggars
looking for free chocolate. *Chocolate!*

Yakima doesn't know chocolate's
as native as the river it banks on.
I can't get righteous. Karen answered
the door, handed out candy. I was

in the kitchen cooking jelly,
made from the wine grapes I planted
20 years ago, to alter memory. I'm listening
to the Stones, '68, music from you. Vance,

the music takes me back to Nam.
It's opening up at last, smoke from burning villes
have turned into smoke signals to God.
The Great Mother nurtures.

The Great Mother eats her young.
It's all love. The New Year:
All Saints' Day was originally the Celtic
celebration of Samhain.

Crops are in. Trick or treat.
Rest in Earth Mother's womb.
Finally, November 2, All Souls' Day,
we celebrate the dead

and freedom for all that dies.
Your photo of the petroglyphs at Canyonlands
goes up on a wall I'm building
with young people, called Palimpsest.

We're exploring how our lives
become layered, how cover-ups happen
naturally, how it's part of the grand design
we spend the rest of our lives stripping

away. Joyful celebration. Vance,
this isn't written up for the School Board.
What do you suppose we'll find in ourselves
this June when we take down the wall? Vance,

your vision burns in me now even
as I cover it up. This is the spirit world.
I call for a picnic at the cemetery. Bring
the camera that lets us play with the shutter.

ANOTHER WAR STORY

—for Tim O'Brien, again

I belonged to the space between two sides.
This was home. I told the army this before
they took my name and gave me a uniform.
Most of what I knew I knew early. I knew
I wouldn't pull their trigger. I knew

my country was the State of North Dakota.
The chaplain, a Lutheran like myself, listened
all through Basic Training before
he told me Lutherans believed in war.
In Vietnam I had rank, and I had mission.

The Catholic Bishop told me
every breath came from God.
Every time Vietnam surfaces in my dream
I turn to Tim O'Brien. Kids ask me, today,
Were you in Woodstock?

I suppose it's the long hair.
I did listen to some of the music.
No, I say, No I wasn't.
I never watched MASH.
My wife would sit in front of the TV laughing.

People at work would talk
about Klinger and Hawkeye
but I knew enough to stay away.
I couldn't feel close to anybody.
O'Brien was the student body president

at a small college with a scholarship

to Harvard and a low draft number.
I was the evac man in the Evac Hospital,
people came to me to go home—
Home isn't what we think it is.

We were young. I was old at 22.
Story after story. From walking away from war,
to what we carry, right to Calley
and how we gave him up,
as he sacrificed himself for us all.

Each magazine emptied into flesh
calling the world to love. This is O'Brien.
This is love. Staying so cool.
Wrapping our love so tight it couldn't
take a hit. Writing through it.

A ferocious sentence.
Greater than the ferocity
of our bullets, the posture
of our protests and denial:
too radical to be heard against

the university and pentagon.
because all we ever were was love.
And our work isn't finished.
I listen to music with a fighter pilot.
I talk with him about wrapping gauze

around children until they turned into prayers.
He needed to see. Music.
O'Brien makes each man's story easier.
We started out as different as that engineer
who turned himself into a professional clown.

THE WOMAN DISCOVERS AMERICA

She watches from her window.
She waits for the green sedan
to come down the hill.
The man drives slow.
He checks the mailbox.
Hears its click.
She knows he will come.
She knows he will not ask questions.

He will hear the click of the keys.
He will hear the click of the ice in a glass.
Six clicks to the grocery store.
His wife's tongue against her teeth.

She has been in the court room.
She has heard them all, all of the clicks.
The clicks in all of the locks.
Which way is sanctuary?
Her way home is through him
and he is gone. This is combat.
Is she a guerrilla? Who is she?
She is surrounded by art and music.

THE MARINE ON THE FREEWAY

—for Gary Higgins

The marine is in traffic.
He rolls up his windows and screams,
Get out of my way. Get out of my fucking way.
The marine runs on curbs, takes secondary roads,
tailgates when he has to. The marine makes this run daily,
47 miles in traffic, from work to home.
Some days it takes 5 minutes,
some days it takes 10, the marine says,
before he finds his anger,
but it's everyday, he finds it. This is traffic.
Yesterday people didn't get out of his way.

The marine has a beer in his hand before breakfast.
He's talking with his friends. Like the old days.
The marine says a marine hit a kid with a rock
walking through the ville. He remembers the screams.
He says, *I'm not the man who threw the rock.*
The marine says, *I kept my humanity.*
The rock is where I drew the line.
I knew things were fucked. I knew I did not throw the rock.
The marine says, *Vietnam was the best year of my life.*

It's Veteran's Day, 1995
The marine came home from Nam in '68,
got loaded every day for eighteen years.
He says he doesn't know how to be honest.
In Vietnam he could put a pistol against the head
of the sleeping guard and chamber a round.
The marine says, *Wake up soldier.*
The marine says life was that simple.

The marine didn't need a union to get things done in Vietnam.
The marine looks out the window.
He sees the mountain. He sees the lake.
The marine is in traffic.
Don't talk to him about the lake.
Don't talk to him about the mountain.
This is not easy for the marine.
He knows what people say about nature.
It's not that simple.
The marine is in traffic.
Traffic is dangerous.
He is passing on the inside lane.
He's between work and home.
He did not throw the rock.
His windows are rolled up.
He's screaming.
He's telling people to get out of his way.

LETTERS FROM VIETNAM

She loved me for the dangers...
—Othello

for Karen on the eve of our 27th Anniversary

And for the intensity of our days.
For every story from the hospital.
For each picture of a child smiling.
Dahlias are love letters from a war zone.

Traded intimacy. Your first pearls.
Perfume from the east. An *ao dai*
cut to my memory of your skin,
leave room here, Mama Sanh for Karen's breasts.

Black silk pants and hand painted shoes
in metallic pinks the colors of exotic fingernails.
And domestic treasures: roses filling
Japanese dinnerware in circles of promise.

Love treasures and letters. Daily letters.
Pictures of me & Louie Santillo holding
the photo of you I still carry in my wallet.
Me and Louie eating provolone cheese from Jersey.

I put it all in the letters. Everything.
I gave you everything I had.
Everything I did, and wanted to do.
The number of people we put on planes,

the names of people who knew your name.

I held nothing back, nothing.
I dug it up, whatever I could find.
I put it down, and put it in the mail.

You loved me for these letters.
And I loved you for loving me.
Years before these dahlias,
years before you blossomed

and we disappeared with the flowers
in the garden, you married me
for these letters, these testaments
to promises, digging, hard-earned treasure.

FESTIVALS OF LIGHT

—for Glenn, Christmas, 1995

The young man's mother
said he died in Vietnam.
He goes to the Wall to see his name.
It's not there. The mother
is trying to tell her son
that she loves him.
How could she figure
he'd drive so far to find a name?

A man goes to see *Platoon.*
Walking out of the theatre
he says he took a wrong turn.
He spends the next six months
in the Vietnam Veteran's Treatment Center.

He says, *This is life.*
It's not about getting straight.
I learned what's written
on that card.
Take a bullet, make a song.

The mother's going to be all right.
And so is the son.
They both have stories.
People who come behind them, now.
They won't care so much for stories.
They'll be more interested
in making money.

LETTER TO REXROTH FROM WILLIAMS RIVER

It took longer than you predicted, Rexroth,
but today at the Falls in Paterson, we renamed the River.
Quite a celebration. Looking for a way in,
we get some help from Pålzsolt Margittai,
a Hungarian making his 56th visit,
who likens this sacred place to a waterfall
behind bars in the old Soviet.
He brought his girlfriend and a video camera.
Her visa expires this weekend
and they're recording man's concentrated
efforts to restrict beauty. He has plenty
to say, but proves to want the poems more,
helps us with cameras and books.
We're here, called by you, to rename the Passaic.
The grafitti is uncomproming,
from *Los 13 Locos de Passaic, Aquí siempre estarémos,*
and we follow in your tradition,
creating sacramental relationships, using
language given to us in paint:
Fuimos, somos, y seremos. The Williams River.
You called it, Rexroth, the river flows in his veins,
our eyes, and time, part of him, part of us.
I'm with Zev Shanken, a Jew from Teaneck,
and his son, Ezra. I've flown in from Yakima,
a West Coast pilgrimage, carrying the copy of *Paterson*
I've been carrying since 1972, twenty-four years, your rare
and beautiful letter to Williams, written in 1952,
a small book of poems by Shanken mapping his life
as a Jewish man, and a jazz poem tracing
my life with the trombone, honoring the work of Ginsberg.
To make a start out of particulars. That's what Zev
said to his son when he asked what made Williams great.

Looking for a way to get closer, no return
rolling up from the chaos,
the Hungarian takes us to where the fence opens
to allow a man passage, and whispering,
Maybe I did that before, I don't know.
A patch of grass fed by the falls. A rock to sit on.
Searching the past for us all.
You give a voice to the woman, Rexroth.
She talks about sick men and factories.
A woman's voice carrying the doctor's vision,
a man writing poems on prescription slips.
Water smashes rock and rises from the Williams River.
Nos vemos. Estamos aquí.

A BEGINNING IN SILK

—for Zev

Binding five poems with silk thread
is a dream from the Chinese. A working dream.
Different coasts, different extremes.
Paterson, at the Great Falls of the Williams River.
Industrial America. One brother makes silk,
The other, the Colt .45. One building.
Before these public waters, we choose upholstery thread,
partly for its dramatic color, partly out of orneriness,
and bind the continent.
Book binding. Naming rivers.
The easiness of it. Looking at the clock I say, Yesterday
I was walking across Brooklyn Bridge with Zev,
we were with Whitman. After crossing the continent
in an afternoon, it seems so easy
to name a river. We know names are changed
in the heart, not by city councils. We know, too,
Rexroth changed this river 50 years ago. Now Zev's poems.
Two men surprised by friendship in middle-age.
Al Het. For the sins. All things valid and confirmed.
We need this. This river, this day, these sins.
They all serve to bind. Great flights of birds!
At the Blue Note, Ray Brown, bass face, summer wind,
blows out lights from 100 yards, gives us a talking point.
Celebrating his 70th, he laughs from his lumber world,
and passes the mantle to Christian McBride.
Let the demon out of the cage , cries Brown.
In Brown's hands bass strings are steel cables
holding up the bridge over the river.
His bridge, his yard. The swing of his line.
Melody obsessed. Joy. Passing the torch.

His bass validates this day, another fire.
Moving into the poems,
Zev is driving, moving in traffic.
Zev at the Blue Note. Zev at the river.
At the Dakota where the security guard might have been.
Strawberry Fields in Central Park.
Israel. *Al Het.* Zev. Rabbi's son.
All things valid and confirmed.
Whenever I pose I betray myself.
Reading to his son by the falls at the Williams River.
Ginsberg, Rexroth, Williams. Kerouac.
All threads. Each a river. *Say it.*

THE CARETAKER FROM NORTH DAKOTA

Maybe it's in genetic memory.

Maybe I carried wild rose
from country cemeteries
in my pant cuffs. I don't know.
I know it took a lifetime
to shake out the grief.
When I woke up
I was pulling weeds, surrounded
by flowers. These weeds are sweet.
They're weeds of forgiveness.
They lead to the final forgiveness.
They all flower. They all root.

These roses aren't the ones
you see on tables in restaurants.
These are old roses. They bloom once.
This one's Slater's Crimson, from China,
named after an English bureaucrat.
Josephine collected this one
in her garden at LaMalaison.
She liked disordered profusion.
Her passion for roses dates from
the year Napoleon became emperor.
These are done for this year,
don't look for blossoms.
They're not all form like the modern teas
that bloom all summer long. The ones
that look like anorexic fashion models
in magazines in Safeway. These roses
bloom once, knock you out with their perfume,
petals turn themselves inside out to open,

and get you all year long with thorns.
They're dangerous. Poison in the beauty.
Desire and thorns.
I learned that here,
on my blessed knees pulling these weeds.
One man's weed is another man's flower.
That's cliché. All weeds flower.
And in the right spot. Remember Lady Bird,
Johnson's wife. She cultivated
the border worlds of wild flowers.
LBJ needed the modern rose
and all the women promised by form.
What he knows about the garden
we know from the way he defoliated Vietnam.

Lady Bird knew the black-eyed Susans
coming up along fence rows,
and purple asters alongside the road.
She had two questions:
How would you get the seeds out?
How would you go about planting?
Mind you, she's talking about weeds.
She lived the world inside the borderline.
Hamlet didn't know flowers or weeds.
Look at his work.
Ophelia only knew flowers.

North Dakota now. You know anybody
who lives in North Dakota?

This isn't romance.
I pull these weeds. I don't want them.
I don't like this spurge.
Spurge has roots halfway to China.

Seeds from May to October.
Prostate all over your garden.
This purslane only looks like moss rose.
It looks like a succulent.
It makes a bed fast. Roots wherever
it touches soil. Pulled,
left on the ground, it reroots.
Puncture vine gets those bicycle tires.
These weeds flower. I weed.
These weeds are built to last.
Nature gave them what they needed.
I weed systematically every week.
And random-systematic while I rake and prune.
Weed is what a caretaker does.

The final forgiveness?
Forgiveness of self.

JEREMIAH'S VOICE

Too much is going on in the garden,
I can't see it, but all this rain,
and the warm days. I can feel
what I can't see. Reading Jeremiah
on Sunday all I hoped for
was to present the word.
Then the word inside my voice
became too strong. I could hardly breathe.
Like my breath took over my voice.
This happened in front of people.
Words I've read all my life.
Karen knew. *What came up in Jeremiah?*
she asked, *It was wonderful.*
I was terrified. This quest for truth.
It won't all go into flowers.
A garden in November
wants a caretaker who can
put things to rest. But God.
God now, wants the people to move.

BLACKBERRY SYRUP

Spooning ice cream through the rich syrup
the berry comes alive, black, tart, clear.
A woman asks about the scratches
on the backs of my hands. The searcher
after the great treasures is always a thief.
I thought the blackberries would disappear,
but I was wrong. It's the forests.
Berries thrive when forests are cut.
Now I am seen for who I am. Preparing
the wild salmon from the Atlantic,
I squeeze a lime over diced garlic.
I add blackberry honey.
Moistened hickory chips piled
by the side of the fish makes a smoke
sweet enough to call up any dream.
The searcher always intrudes.
Chunks of pepper lodged in my teeth
give me a dose of my own medicine.
Deep water filet. Pink flesh.
A personal feast. Things most aberrant
are what I have been called to do.
All my sins, necessary.
Invited here all along. To dangerous vines,
enticed to the treasure, handed my dice.
Syrup warms the cool cream.
Towards the meal no one can believe in.

About the Author:

Jim Bodeen is editor, printer, publisher of Blue Begonia Press.
He lives with his wife Karen.
He is the Keeper of the Poetry Pole in the garden.
He runs with the black lab retriever Lacy Dreamwalker.

The Artist says:

The shield is made of paper, silk and light wood.
The material is frail, the spirit can be strong.
You will have to catch it yourself.

Marty Lovins

The Photographer says:

I am a teacher.
I am a photographer.
I photograph to see and to share what I see with others.
I teach photography to encourage students in their seeing and their sharing.

Rob Prout